THE GHOSTLY TALES OF CLEVELAND

Published by Arcadia Children's Books
A Division of Arcadia Publishing
Charleston, SC
www.arcadiapublishing.com

First published 2021

ISBN 9781540249258

Library of Congress Control Number: 2021938344

All images courtesy of Shutterstock.com; p. 40 Nina Alizada/Shutterstock.com; p. 54 Barbara Kalbfleisch/Shutterstock.com; p. 64 Kenneth Sponsler/Shutterstock.com; p. 100 Showcase Imaging/Shutterstock.com

Spooky America

The Ghostly Tales of Cleveland

BETH A. RICHARDS

ıpted from *Haunted Cleveland* by Beth A. Richards and Chuck L. Gove

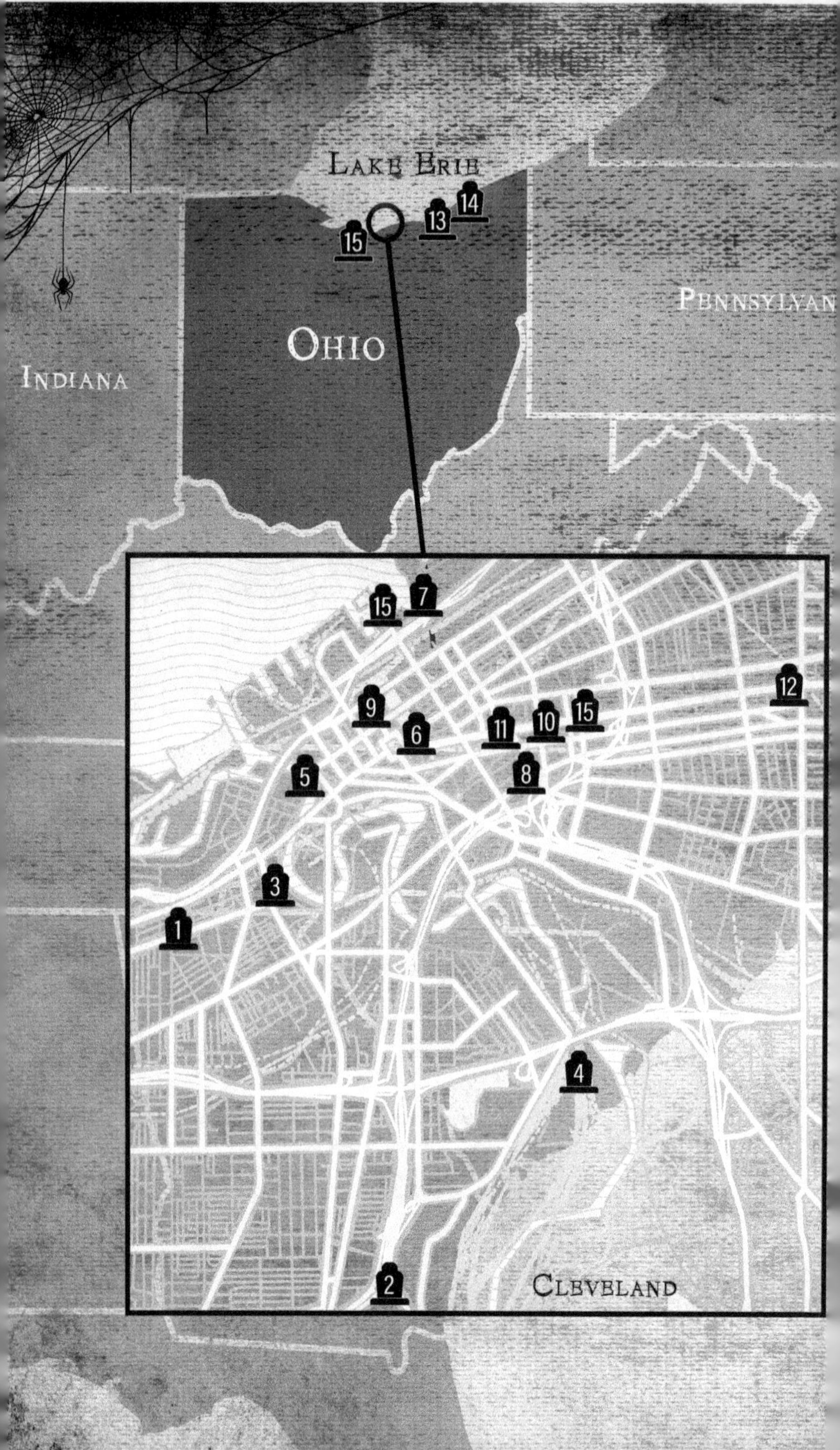
Lake Erie
Ohio
Indiana
Pennsylvan
Cleveland
15
13
14
15
7
9
6
11
10
15
12
5
8
3
1
4
2

Table of Contents & Map Key

Introduction 2

1 Chapter 1. Franklin Castle 5

2 Chapter 2. Riverside Cemetery 13

3 Chapter 3. Robert Russell Rhodes Mansion 21

4 Chapter 4. The Midwest Railway Preservation Society 27

5 Chapter 5. The Powerhouse 35

6 Chapter 6. Soldiers' and Sailors' Monument 41

7 Chapter 7. USS *Cod* 49

8 Chapter 8. Erie Street Cemetery .55

9 Chapter 9. The Cleveland Police Museum 59

10 Chapter 10. Playhouse Square 65

11 Chapter 11. Grays Armory 73

12 Chapter 12. The Cleveland Agora 83

13 Chapter 13. Squire's Castle 89

14 Chapter 14. Fairport Harbor Marine Museum and Lighthouse. . . .95

15 Chapter 15. Around the Town Ghosts 101

Introduction

Hopefully you have heard of Cleveland, Ohio. It is the second largest city in Ohio and has the second largest theater district in the country (after New York City), as well as world-renowned museums. If you're a sports fan, you know it's home to the Browns football team, the Cavaliers basketball team, and the (soon to be renamed) Indians baseball team. And Cleveland has a rich history that has earned the city the nickname, "the Best Location in the Nation."

Moses Cleaveland and his team of surveyors arrived at the mouth of the Cuyahoga River on July 22, 1796. They established a settlement there and named it after their leader. Moses went back to his home in Connecticut and never returned to the settlement that was named after him. The city of Cleveland was incorporated December 23, 1814, and early settler Lorenzo Carter made Cleveland a trading post and became one of the city's first policemen. (Fun fact: the original spelling of Cleveland was Cleaveland, but in 1831, a newspaper dropped the "a" so it fit on the page better. The name stuck, but the newspaper didn't.

Today, Cleveland is a must-see city, not only due to its incredible history, but also because of all the incredible things you can see and do there. And that just happens to include ghosts. Bet you didn't know that one of the most awesome things about Cleveland is our ghosts! And being a tour guide for Haunted Cleveland Ghost Tours means that I've had the pleasure (and the fright) of meeting some of the city's ghosts.

Franklin Castle

Looming eerily over Franklin Boulevard on Cleveland's west side is a home called Franklin Castle. Considered the most haunted house in Cleveland, it was built for Hannes Tiedemann and his family. Construction started on this massive gray sandstone four-story home in 1881 and was finished between late 1882 and early 1883. The house has a tower, a fourth-floor ballroom, a wine cellar, and about thirty rooms. It was home to Hannes, his wife Luise, and their children. Hannes's mother also stayed with the family for long periods of time.

Hannes and Luise had a son and daughter, August and Emma, and they had lost three other children who died shortly after they were born. The family enjoyed the first few years in the home, but then tragedy struck. In 1891, when she was 15 years old, Emma died from complications from diabetes, and then Hannes's mother passed away not long after that. It's said that Luise Tiedemann began to redecorate the house to cheer herself up after these sad events. Legend has it that this is when the hidden rooms and secret passages were added to the home.

There were a lot of rumors about Hannes Tiedemann. One of the stories claims that he became angry with one of his servants, a woman named Rachel, and he strangled her to death in the tower room. Later occupants of the house reported hearing the sound of a woman choking in the upstairs tower room, and many people claim they have seen a woman in black standing at the window in that room.

Hannes is also rumored to have killed a girl in the ballroom, and there are many reports of supernatural things happening in that space. One woman reported that when she was at the top of the stairs leaving the ballroom, something pushed her from behind; lucky for her, she was holding the handrail.

Luise passed away in 1895. Years later, a newspaper delivery boy was delivering the morning paper to Franklin Castle. It was very early and still dark as he opened the gate and started to walk up the front walk. As he reached the front door, a woman in a white dress floated through it. The paperboy stopped dead in his tracks and watched her drift past him and down the front walk, where she disappeared in front of his eyes. When he could finally move, he ran all the way home and quit his paper route that day. Most people think that the woman in white is the ghost of Luise Tiedemann.

Hannes sold the house in 1896, and the creepy stories stopped for a while, until the Romano family bought the house in 1968. They planned to turn it into a bed and breakfast—and that's when the ghostly activity started up again. The Romano kids asked their mom if they could take cookies to the little girl upstairs crying; they said she was wearing an old-fashioned dress and seemed really sad. Mrs. Dolores Romano heard organ music playing in the house—the organ had been taken out of the house years earlier. She also heard voices coming from empty rooms, perhaps paranormal echoes of the past. The story goes that the Romano family moved out

of Franklin Castle because their priest was afraid that something in the house was going to hurt them.

Around 1975, a local radio host, John Webster, came to the castle to do a special Halloween radio show. When he went upstairs, his tape recorder was ripped off his shoulder and thrown down the stairs. After the broadcast, he listened to the play back of the show. He was terrified to hear a sinister laugh in the background—the laugh could only be heard on the recording.

I can't tell you if all these stories are true, but I can tell you about my personal ghostly experiences at Franklin Castle. One year, my Haunted Cleveland partner Chuck and I were invited by the caretaker to spend the night before Halloween and do a live radio show from the castle. The night started out great. We filmed all over the castle and finally, Chuck, the caretaker, and I settled down for the night in the front room. Chuck was the last to fall asleep. He had just dozed off when he heard two people talking right outside the room. He thought we had woken up and got up to see what we were doing. To his surprise, the two of us were still asleep. He did the most sensible thing he could think of: he laid back down and pulled the blanket over his head! I guess that is one way to hide from ghosts!

When we used to take people on tours through the castle, we split up the group. I would stay outside with half the group and tell them the legends about the castle, and the other group would tour the house. One night I was telling the story of Luise Tiedemann, the woman in white floating through the door. And suddenly, I was pushed from behind! It wasn't a hard push, but it was hard enough that I took a step forward. At first, I thought it was one of our tour group, but I turned around to see that there was no one behind me. That was the last time I told the story of the lady in white while I was standing outside the castle!

Recently, while the house was being renovated, we were lucky enough to talk to some of the construction workers. One of them said that someone or something liked to hide their tools and would occasionally send bricks flying around the room. Scary stuff!

The caretaker who lives in Franklin Castle during the winter months has told me that he has heard some unexplained noises during the night and footsteps echoing through the house, but the paranormal activity in the house has slowed down for the most part. It's almost as if all the spirits in the house like what's happening in their home now. But I would watch what stories you tell around the castle—you never know who is listening.

Riverside Cemetery

Riverside Cemetery is located on Cleveland's west side. It covers over one hundred acres and is a very beautiful place. Before it opened in 1876, there were no cemeteries on the west side, and people who lived on that side of town had to bury their dead on the east side. That meant they had to cross a bridge and pay a toll.

There is a small stone chapel in the cemetery. It is the only original building on the property. Underneath the chapel is a vault that can store up to thirty coffins. The vault was used mainly in the winter when the ground was frozen and it was too difficult to dig graves by hand. The red sandstone office, located at the entrance of the cemetery, was built in 1896 and is in the National Historic Register.

Over the years, many of Cleveland's important citizens have been laid to rest in the cemetery, including John Richardson, the architect who designed Franklin Castle; the Rhodes family (who we will read about in a later chapter); and Harry Farnsworth, who developed the Cleveland Metro Park System. There is also an area in the cemetery dedicated to people who donated their body to science. After scientists are done with the bodies, they are buried in a special section of Riverside Cemetery.

Now, we just read about Franklin Castle and the original owners, the Tiedemann family. Well, Riverside Cemetery is the final resting place for the family. And it seems that the ghost of Hannes Tiedemann likes to make an appearance from time to time. People have told stories about an older man standing at the front gate of the cemetery. When asked if he needs help, he says he wants to see his daughter and asks for a ride home to Franklin Boulevard. As the car gets to Franklin Castle, the old man simply disappears! Can you imagine driving a ghost around? I have given tours in this cemetery for many years, and I have never seen the spirit of Hannes Tiedemann, but if I did, I can tell you I would definitely pick him up!

Ghost hunters often use copper dowsing rods to pick up ghost energy and communicate with spirits, and we have had our guests use them in the cemetery. One night, a woman was using the dowsing rods and walking in the direction the rods were pointing. Suddenly they stopped moving—and she found herself standing in front of a gravestone that had her last name on it. What a shock! The guest never knew she had relatives buried at Riverside, and she believed her relative's spirit brought her to their grave. She had a friend take a picture of her standing by the grave, and in the photo, there was a large orb (a ball of spirit energy) right above her hands. Pretty cool that the ghost guiding her wanted to be in the picture, too!

When we first wanted to take ghost hunters through Riverside, we had to clear it with Ken Langley, the caretaker, since he would need to open the gates for us. Ken was happy to help out, but what we didn't know at that time was that Ken and his family lived on the property. Ken had two young daughters, Ashley and Amanda, who wanted to help out. The only problem is they didn't tell us they wanted to help out.

On our first night at Riverside, I told stories at the Tiedemann graves and then let the group explore the cemetery as I went back to

the bus. One of our guests came back and asked who the bride and groom were walking around the cemetery. I replied that I had no idea, but maybe there was a wedding in the chapel. The woman laughed, saying it was kind of creepy, and she got back on the bus. More guests started to come back, all of them commenting on the bride and groom.

I will be honest that I was pretty happy to be leaving the cemetery. I was wary of that ghostly couple who had walked through the cemetery and then just disappeared. We stopped to thank Ken, and he pulled me aside and said, "I hope you don't mind but my daughters were so excited and they wanted to dress up to help with the tour." I started to laugh and said, "Oh, no. It was great. I knew it was them the whole time." Of course I did *not* know it was Amanda and Ashley, but there was no need for anyone to know the "ghosts" had freaked me out!

Riverside Cemetery is a great place to visit and explore the history of the folks who have lived and died in Cleveland. But if you see a ghostly bride and groom, I can't say for sure if it's Ashley and Amanda!

Robert Russell Rhodes Mansion

Down the street from Franklin Castle, at 2905 Franklin Boulevard, is an enormous red stone mansion. Built in 1874, this was originally the home of Robert Russell Rhodes, a successful businessman who inherited his father's many businesses. Robert Rhodes sold his home in 1888 and moved to Lakewood, Ohio.

The mansion was bought by Cuyahoga County in 1914, and the county has used it for many things over the years. It was a juvenile detention center from 1918 to 1923, and from 1939 to 1962, it served as a nursing home. After that, it became a school for disabled children from 1963 until 1977.

In 1977, the red stone mansion became the county archive building. This building held all the county records of marriages, births, and deaths, and there was a research room where people could look up their family histories. At that time, the county connected the Rhodes Mansion and the Sanford House next door. The Sanford House part of the property was used by the Western Reserve Historical Society.

Because the building has had so many uses and so many people have come through its doors, it is easy to believe some people have decided to stay on—even after death. One of those ghosts is a young boy. I think we can assume he must have roamed the building when it was a juvenile detention center or a school. Staff members have reported seeing him reflected in a mirror in the basement restroom. They all tell the same story: when they look in the mirror, they see a young boy in overalls standing behind them, but when they turn around, they are all alone! They also tell stories about hearing a ball being bounced down the stairs.

Along with his ball playing, it is reported that sometimes the young boy would get a little cranky. When he felt he was not getting enough attention, he would head into the

research room where people were working on genealogy projects and swing the chandelier from side to side. Apparently, the only way they could get him to stop is to yell at him to cut it out! People who used this room say the building's resident ghost also hid their research notes and moved their things around.

One of the night security guards had quite a few stories about his young ghostly companion. The security guard admits that while working the "graveyard shift," he had maybe fallen asleep on the job a few times. But he was always woken up by the sound of the building alarm or lights flashing on and off. The security guard said when he first started working there, his ghostly coworker freaked him out a little bit. But after a while, he just appreciated the help he had staying awake on the job.

Another security guard told a story about one night during a shift change. The rule was that both guards had to go through the whole building together. When they got to the elevator, they heard the elevator running. Not so unusual you might say, except for the fact that it was after hours, no one else was there, and oh yeah, the elevator system had not worked for years! But it gets even weirder—they heard a little boy talking. So the officers did the only sensible thing. They finished their search in record time and rushed outside! The officer who was going on duty said, "Well, you may as well lock that door. I am not going back in there tonight; I will keep watch from my car." And that's what he did; he sat in his locked car all night in the parking lot. Can you really blame him?

The Midwest Railway Preservation Society

Did you think ghosts only haunt houses? Not here in Cleveland! The Midwest Railway Preservation Society actually has a haunted rail car called "the Death Car." The name itself is pretty scary, so wait until you hear the stories about it!

Located in the area of downtown Cleveland known as The Flats is the historical B&O

Roundhouse. The building was originally used from 1905 to 1919 by the Baltimore & Ohio (B&O) Railroad.

In 1955, the Midwest Railway Preservation Society bought the rundown building and is now dedicated to restoring locomotives, train cars, and the roundhouse itself. A roundhouse is a circular or semicircular building with stalls where locomotives can be parked to be repaired or stored. There is usually a turntable that is used to turn the engines around when the work is done.

On August 30, 1943, a passenger train in traveling through Wayland, New York, was involved in a horrible accident with a freight train. The freight train had ignored a stop signal and moved onto the same track the passenger train was traveling on. The engineer of the freight train was behind schedule and trying to make up time. Up ahead, the passenger train pulled onto the track in front of the speeding freight train, not aware of how fast the freight train was going. There was no time to stop, and the two trains collided. During the crash, some cars derailed, but one car, the Death Car, slid on the tracks and split the boiler of the freight train's locomotive. The crash blew out the windows of the passenger car and sent boiling water and steam all over the passengers. According to the official report, twenty-six people were instantly killed, two others died later of their injuries, and one hundred fourteen were injured, six of whom were from Cleveland. Some of these poor souls who died that day seem not to have given up their seats on the train and like to make themselves known to volunteers and visitors.

The Death Car was brought by train to Cleveland in 2013, and the Midwest Railway Preservation Society started renovating the railway car. While painters were working on it, they opened all the windows to get the paint smell out. But the windows kept closing on their own. They thought maybe because the windows were so old, they just kept sliding down, so they propped them open

with sticks. They kept on painting until, all of a sudden, there was a loud bang, and all the windows slammed shut at the same time! They quit painting for the day, and I can't say I blame them.

Many visitors to the Death Car have seen a man in old-fashioned clothes and hat sitting on top of the car, just swinging his legs over the side. Steve, one of the volunteers at the society, has led many tours through the car. Sometimes after finishing his talk people, people would ask if the man standing behind him had any stories to tell. The hair would stand up on the back of Steve's neck because he knew exactly who this man was.

When we took tour groups through the Death Car, I know at least one person had a really strange experience. A volunteer named Charlie started to tell the history of the car, and before he even got to the accident, one of the guests started to get very hot and was having trouble breathing. I helped her outside, and she felt better right away. I think she may have been reliving the experience of those people trapped in the car during the horrible accident.

Charlie, the volunteer, also told us a story about a B&O Railroad worker who had died in the roundhouse. Volunteers feel that his spirit is still there. The ghost of the railway worker likes to move tools, and volunteers often hear someone whistling, even when they are working by themselves. One night when we were in the roundhouse, Charlie had just finished his story about this spirit when I saw a man in our group jump and look around. He seemed a little freaked out. I caught up with him and asked if he was having a good time. He said yes, but while he was listening to the story, he thought his wife was right behind him, tapping him on the shoulder. When he looked around, his wife was next to him, and no one was behind him. He started to take pictures, and in every picture, there was a shadowy figure.

The Midwest Railway Preservation Society is open for tours, so you can check out the Death Car yourself, and keep your eyes and ears open for those passengers who have yet to reach their final destination . . .

The Powerhouse

The Powerhouse

In downtown Cleveland, on the west bank of the Cuyahoga River, there are lots of old factories, giant brick buildings that used to be home to manufacturing businesses. One of the buildings, erected in 1892, is now known as "the Powerhouse." It comes by its name honestly because it used to supply all the power to the streetcar lines that ran through the city.

The Powerhouse is now home to restaurants, a party center, and the Cleveland Aquarium.

This building was designed by John Richardson, the same architect who designed Franklin Castle. He wanted it to look like factories in Europe, so it has large chimneys and giant windows.

The city's streetcars lost out to automobiles, so, in 1920, the streetcars were taken out of service, and so was the Powerhouse. It stayed empty for many years, but in 1989, it was renovated for use as office space and an entertainment spot.

The night security guards at the Powerhouse have some of the best stories, and one security guard told me that one of the businesses has a very tidy ghost in their office. If anyone leaves a drawer open, the conscientious spirit in the office will close it. One worker decided it would be funny to leave as many drawers as possible open in their office and started to walk out of the room. However, the ghost didn't think it was very funny and slammed all the drawers shut. No one has tried that experiment again.

Another guard told a story about the Powerhouse, which started when he was a

kid. He grew up around the Powerhouse and was always interested in the building. It was already empty at that point, and he and his friends would sneak in and play there (which probably wasn't a very good idea). The building was pretty run down, and the lower level was flooded. When a construction company drained the lower level before the next renovation, they found something shocking—a car with a body inside. Even though this guard and his friends had to stop exploring the Powerhouse once construction started, his interest in the building continued. So when he got older and saw an ad that the property needed security guards, he applied for a job right away.

The guard said that late at night, when all the visitors have gone home and the building is empty, he hears voices and the sound of machinery. He believes he's hearing what the building was like in its heyday, when it supplied power to the streetcars. On the lower level, the faucets in the bathrooms turn on and off and the toilets flush on their own. When he goes to check, he knows no one will be there, but he goes anyway. Who knew that ghosts need bathroom breaks?

The Cuyahoga County Soldiers' and Sailors' Monument

Soldiers' and Sailors' Monument

Located at 3 Public Square, right in the center of downtown Cleveland, is the Soldiers' and Sailors' Monument. The monument was dedicated on July 4, 1894, and was erected to honor the soldiers from Cuyahoga County who served during the Civil War. It was designed by Captain Levi Scofield, and he took the job on one condition: that he would not be paid for his work.

Captain Scofield designed a very unusual monument. It did not glorify the war; instead, it glorified the service of the men and women in Cuyahoga County. The four statues on the memorial represent the four branches of the Union forces: the Army, the Navy, the cavalry, and the infantry. Inside the monument, the bronze reliefs on the walls show the Soldiers Aid Society, the women's group that raised money for the war effort; the Emancipation of Slaves; Beginning of the War in Ohio; and the End of the War. One of the most unusual design choices that Captain Scofield made was including the contributions that women made to the war effort.

The statue on top of the 125-foot column is the Goddess of Freedom, a woman holding a sword, and Captain Scofield used his own wife as a model. She modeled for the statue in Scofield's own uniform and actually held his sword. There are marble tablets on the walls containing the names and regiment of every soldier from Cuyahoga County who served in the Civil War.

The monument is an amazing place to visit, and we are always happy to share this history with our tour groups. But even more exciting than sharing the monument's history is sharing what lies beneath—secret tunnels! One of the guides at the monument, Tim Leslie, and some local ghost hunting groups have been lucky enough to have some ghostly encounters at the monument.

One day while Tim was working, a visitor came up to Tim. He said he was a Vietnam veteran, and he was able to see ghosts. He told Tim he could see the ghost

of a man in full Civil War uniform standing just inside the door, and it seemed like the ghost was standing guard. Tim said he got goosebumps every time he walked through the door after that!

Another time, a local ghost hunting group was given permission to do an investigation in the tunnels, and Tim served as their guide. The group wanted to do an EVP (electronic voice phenomenon) session with a digital voice recorder. Ghost hunters often use a digital voice recorder to communicate with spirits; they ask spirits questions and hopefully record their answers. As Tim led the group through the tunnels, they had their recorder going, and he asked, "Is there anyone here who wants to speak to us?" The group continued asking questions, and when they finished, they went back upstairs to review the evidence. When they listened to the recording, they could hear a woman's voice saying, "They are coming. They are here." Creepy! Then they heard Tim ask if anyone wanted to talk, and again they heard a woman's voice. This time she stated, "I am Carrie." One of the investigators looked at the names underneath the bronze relief of the Ladies Aid Society, and sure enough, one of the women was named Carrie Grant! Have you got goosebumps yet?

Some people have a "ghost app" on their phones and use it as another way to talk to spirits. One night during a tour, the phone of someone who had the app started saying "Elizabeth" over and over again. It was very weird, especially when you find out that the name of Captain Scofield's wife was Elizabeth.

One night when we got to the Soldiers' and Sailors' Monument, Tim looked like he was kind of freaked out. I asked him if everything was okay, and he told me this story. He had been down in the tunnel, checking on lights, when he felt someone grab his arm. He looked around, and he was by himself. Tim's arm suddenly started to burn, and when he pulled up his sleeve, he saw three scratches. Who—or what—could have or would have done that? That night we stayed with him at the momument until he had locked up.

One of the stranger things happened in the memorial room. Because the tunnels are so small, we often split up groups. On one tour, I was gathering the group who was to head to the tunnels. A woman got in the line to file down the stairs. She said, "Excuse me. You never introduced the nice young man in uniform who was telling me stories. Does he work for you?" I looked around and said, "No, ma'am, we don't have anyone else work for us." She looked around and said quietly, "Then who was I talking to?" The woman quickly got out of line and headed to the bus, and to be honest, I wanted to go with her!

The monument is open for tours, and don't be scared if you visit and the spirit of a long-dead soldier reaches out to get your attention!

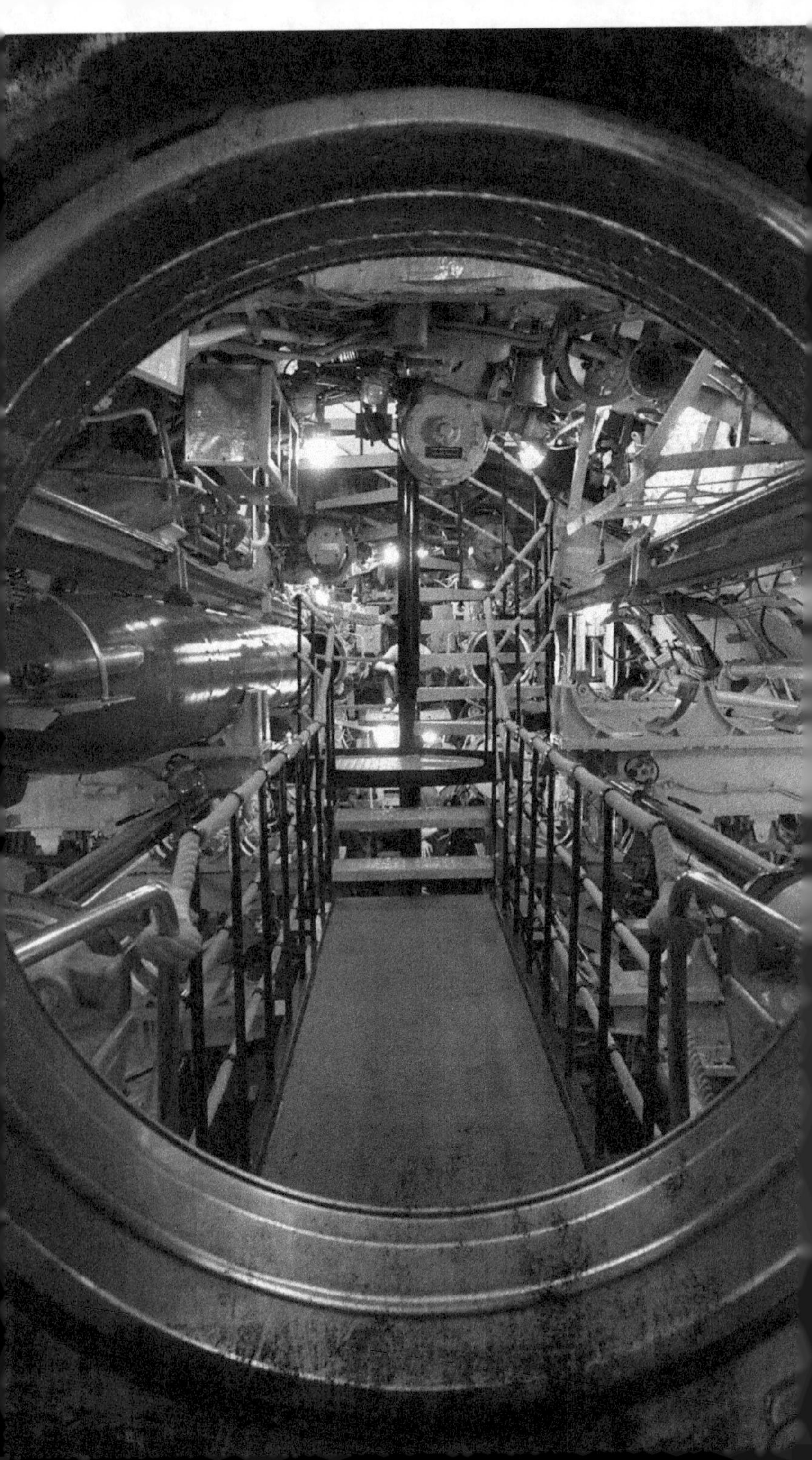

USS *Cod*

Docked on the shore of Lake Erie in downtown Cleveland is the USS *Cod*. This submarine was launched on March 21, 1943, and is in the National Historic Register. It is now a museum that Clevelanders are lucky to have.

The USS *Cod* was used during World War II to fight the enemy in the South Pacific. It made seven successful patrols, with a total of four hundred fifteen patrol days before the war ended. The *Cod* claimed to have sunk ten enemy vessels—and damaged another five—with its torpedoes.

The *Cod*'s claim to fame came on its last patrol. On July 8, 1945, the submarine helped a Dutch submarine that had run aground in enemy waters. The *Cod* tried to tow the Dutch sub off a reef for two days. It was then that the crew realized the only way to save the Dutch sailors was to bring all 56 of them onboard the *Cod* and make their way to safety. So for three days, the *Cod* was home to 153 men (that's a lot for a sub!) as they made their way back to safe waters.

There was only one wartime death aboard the *Cod*, and that happened in April 1945. The *Cod* was getting ready to leave on its sixth patrol in enemy waters, and one member of the crew, named Andrew Johnson, was really nervous. He was not afraid of the enemy; he was terrified because he believed he was cursed. Andrew was afraid that his curse would harm the whole crew. He told other crew members that his grandfather and father had died before their 27th birthday and he knew that he was doomed to follow in their footsteps. Unfortunately, Andrew's 27th birthday was in June, when the *Cod* would be on patrol.

On the night of April 27, 1945, an electric battery that charged the torpedoes had a short, which started a fire inside a torpedo. If the torpedo completely caught fire, it would explode, causing the sub to sink and most likely kill the crew.

The first two sailors on the scene were Larry Fully and Andrew Johnson. Two other sailors soon joined them, and they were able to fire the torpedo, saving the crew. But before Fully and Johnson could get down below, a huge wave swept over the sub, washing them overboard and out to sea.

The crew searched all night for the two men, and finally at dawn, just before the captain was ready to give up the search they found Larry Fully. He told the rest of the crew that he held onto Andrew until a wave pulled them apart. Before Larry could swim back to him, Andrew went under the water and disappeared.

Sadly, Andrew Johnson did fall victim to his family "curse" and died before his 27th birthday. But the crew of the *Cod* feels like Andrew Johnson is still watching over the submarine. They hear footsteps above them when there's no way anyone could be walking there. Lights on the sub turn off and on, and bells ring—perhaps Andrew signaling them that they need to do something. The crew is not afraid of Andrew's spirit; they are happy he is there helping them out.

Do we have any proof that the spirit of Andrew Johnson walks the deck of the *Cod*? Nope, but if you're on the sub and lights start blinking and bells start ringing, it may be a coincidence or it may just be Andrew's way of saying hello.

Joc-O-Sot's gravestone, Erie Street Cemetery

Erie Street Cemetery

Across the street from Progressive Field, where the Cleveland Indians play, is Erie Street Cemetery, the oldest existing cemetery in Cleveland. The cemetery was established in 1826, and Minerva White was the first person buried there, in September 1827.

Over the years, the cemetery has had some problems with vandals and grave robbers, but the most famous headstone that was "vandalized" was not the work of criminals. Legend has it that it was done by the person buried beneath it, Chief Joc-O-Sot!

Chief Joc-O-Sot was a Sauk Indian chief who fought and was wounded in the 1832 Black Hawk War. He came to Cleveland and worked as a hunting and fishing guide and then became a member of a vaudeville troupe called the Dan Marble Theatrical Group. The group toured the United States and Europe and even met Queen Victoria in 1844.

Joc-O-Sot was very sick at the end of the European tour and tried to get back to Cleveland, but he never made it home. His body was returned to Cleveland and buried at Erie Street Cemetery.

The people who were with Joc-O-Sot when he died said he wanted to be buried with his tribe, but that didn't happen. And apparently because of that, it is said his spirit can't rest.

The legend is that Chief Joc-O-Sot was so angry, that his spirit knocked over and smashed his original gravestone. A new headstone was put up in hopes that would appease his spirit—but it didn't. Chief Joc-O-Sot continues to haunt the cemetery, and he's even been seen across the street at Progressive Field.

If you happen to be in Erie Street Cemetery at night and you see a tall, dark shadow lingering near the shattered headstone of Chief Joc-O-Sot, you may want to turn around and head back the way you came!

The Cleveland Police Museum

The Cleveland Police Museum was the idea of Detective Robert Bolton. He came up with the idea after visiting Scotland Yard's Black Museum in London. In 1983, the Cleveland Police Historical Society was formed, and the organization opened the museum that same year.

The society has some amazing exhibits in the museum, which include the history of the Cleveland Police, as well as Cleveland's mafia.

Now, I'm sure you're saying, the history of the Cleveland Police is great, but where's the ghost? Many ghost hunters believe that spirits can travel with objects they are attached to. So when things come into the museum, they may have a ghost hitching a ride.

One of the exhibits in the museum includes a jail cell that came from the women's division of the old Central Police Station, which was the police headquarters, police court, and jail from 1863 through 1893. One afternoon, the president of the museum stopped by for a visit, and he spotted a woman walking around, looking at the exhibits. When she got to the jail cell, he heard her gasp. As he turned around, she fainted and fell to the floor. She was only out for a few seconds, and the president of the museum got her up and asked her if she was okay. She was embarrassed and said that the woman in the jail cell, who she described as middle-aged and wearing a long gray dress, had surprised her. She thought she was the only visitor in the museum at the time. Well, she was the only *living* visitor in the museum!

A few weeks later, a group of senior citizens came in for a tour and two of them went up to one of the museum volunteers and asked why there was a woman locked in the jail cell? When they described her, they said she was (you guessed it!) a middle-aged woman dressed in a long gray dress. When the volunteer went over to check the jail cell, it was empty. But the door was closed and locked, which was strange because the door is always kept open with a lock and chain so that no kids smash their fingers. The chain was just hanging there, swinging on the bar! Did this ghost travel with the cell? It certainly seems like this woman was locked up for life (and death).

In 2012, the museum started a new exhibit called, "Capital Punishment in Cuyahoga

County." This exhibit told the history of the electric chair, as well as the story of nine men who were sentenced to death. Included in the exhibit was the only electric chair that was ever used in Ohio, loaned by the Ohio Historical Society. A barrier was put around the chair so that visitors could not get that close to it.

A retired attorney came in to visit the capital punishment exhibit, only to hurry back to the front of the museum to tell the volunteer on duty that there was a man in a gray shirt and pants sitting in the chair. Of course, by the time they got back over to the chair, it was empty.

Right before the exhibit was scheduled to close, a group of school kids came in for a tour. As they got to the electric chair, they noticed a woman standing inside the barrier. One of the kids asked a worker in the gift shop if they could go inside the barrier. The worker ran over to the exhibit and saw that there was no one there. She asked the kids what the person looked like, thinking they might say a man dressed in gray. Imagine her surprise when they said it was an older woman dressed in gray!

When the museum started to take down the exhibit, the staff was checking the chair over to make sure it was okay before they returned it to the historical society. Stuck to the leg of the chair was a piece of gray cloth. No one can swear it wasn't there the whole time, but it was kind of creepy when both "people" seen near the chair were wearing gray clothes.

Were these two unfortunate souls attached to the electric chair, doomed to sit in it for eternity? Nobody really knows, but what they do know is they haven't been spotted at the museum since the electric chair left. However, the woman locked in the cell is another story! She still lingers in the museum, and you may be lucky enough to see her if you go visit.

Playhouse Square, Cleveland's theater district

Playhouse Square

Playhouse Square, Cleveland's theater district, is the second largest in the country, after New York City, and is a bright light in the city. And the Cleveland theater district is lucky enough to have not one, but two haunted theaters within the complex of five theaters.

Playhouse Square is located in downtown Cleveland at Euclid Avenue and Fourteenth Street. Originally built in the 1920s, Playhouse

Square was a huge part of Cleveland society. The two theaters that have ghostly inhabitants were both opened in 1921. The State Theater opened in February 1921, and the Hanna Theater opened in March.

These amazing theaters offered Clevelanders everything from movies and vaudeville shows to the latest in plays and musicals. But by 1969, all the theaters except the Hanna were closed. Vandals and a fire almost destroyed the others, and there was talk about tearing them down. Then in the early 1980s, there was a renewed interest in saving these buildings.

So are you ready for some theater ghosts? Of course you are! Theaters are notorious for being haunted, and those in Playhouse Square are no different.

One of the ghosts seems to haunt a stairway in the State Theater that goes downstairs to the ladies room. Many women have spoken about a female spirit who brushed up against them as they made their way down the stairs. Some women say that they felt like someone was watching them while they were in the lounge portion of the restroom. On tours, I have seen quite a few women hurrying out of the restroom and up those stairs!

There's another spirit at the State Theater who likes to shake things up! People claim to have seen the ghost of a man in a green suit and green hat on the stage, up in the balcony, and on the lobby staircase. Sometimes he doesn't fully appear, so you may just see some green legs walking past you or a green hat floating by. Once, a wedding party was having their pictures taken on the staircase, and to the bride's surprise, when she looked to see who was standing next to her, all she saw was two legs dressed in green pants! She screamed and ran out of the building. No word if he showed up in the wedding pictures.

I had my own experience in the State Theater one night. I was giving a tour to some students, and while I was standing in an aisle speaking with one of the teachers, someone pushed past me. I was a little surprised that one of the students had pushed past, but when I turned around, there was no one there. Just then, one of the students brought over his camera and showed me a picture he had taken. The picture revealed a man in a green suit standing a few rows away from me, looking a little angry. I believe he was trying to tell me it was time to take this tour out of his theater.

There have been more than a few sightings of the woman in white who roams the Hanna Theater. People believe it is the ghost of a woman who was in an accident on her way home from the theater, and her spirit returned to the last place she had been. Carol, a woman who was in charge of ticket sales at the Hanna, was terrified of ghosts. She had heard the stories, but she really liked her job, so every morning when she got to work, Carol would say to herself, "Please don't let me see the ghost; I love this job, so please don't let me see her." This mantra must have worked, because Carol went to work every day and never had any problems. Until one day, a woman came in to arrange some group tickets. While they were talking, the woman asked, "Have you ever heard that this theater is haunted?" Carol replied, "I have heard stories but never seen anything." The woman then said she was a psychic and the spirit of a woman was standing right behind Carol. Carol panicked until the woman said, "Don't worry. She knows you love this job, and she will never bother you or let you see her." Carol was stunned. She had never told anyone what she said to herself.

But just because Carol never saw this ghost doesn't mean she never made herself known to others. And apparently this female spirit is a bit of a jokester, and she has played a few jokes on some of the actresses during shows. The ghost would switch costumes around, moving them from one dressing room to another. She liked to tangle up their jewelry, and she really liked turning the lights on and off in their dressing rooms. The actresses got used to her tricks and learned to start getting ready for their performances a little bit early!

Playhouse Square is a great place to see a play or a musical and people are just *dying* to get in!

Grays Armory

Grays Armory

If you walk through downtown Cleveland, you may come across a giant red stone fortress, complete with a tower, enormous wooden doors, and an iron gate. If you have, then you have found the home and museum of the Cleveland Grays. The Cleveland Grays (originally known as the Cleveland City Guard) were founded in 1837. They were a wealthy, civic-minded group of citizens who pledged to help local police and be the first line of defense in case Cleveland came under attack. I am not sure who was attacking Cleveland, but the Grays were ready to help.

These ex-military men had served as a group in the Civil War, the Spanish-American War, and their last active service group fought in World War I. Their first meeting was on August 28, 1937, and by the middle of September, seventy-eight men had signed up. In their first year, they changed their name from the Cleveland City Guard to the Cleveland Grays, because their uniforms were gray. The dress uniform was quite unusual and included a very tall black bearskin hat.

The fortress on Bolivar Avenue is enormous! It was completed in May 1893, and it was used for Gray's meetings, recreation, drills, and important society functions. It is four stories high and has a five-story tower. (You can see

Lake Erie from the tower.) The main entrance has a heavy iron gate that can be pulled down in case of danger, and all the windows on the first floor are covered with iron bars. The building has a giant drill hall, which was used for training; meeting rooms; a pool room; a mess hall; a third-floor ballroom; and a shooting range in the basement.

I know, I know, this is all great, but let's get to the good stuff. In a building this old, there has to be a spirit or two wandering the halls, right?

Of course there are! Some of the spirits who roam Grays Armory seem to be there to make sure the armory is being kept up to the high standards of the Cleveland Grays. Other spirits just seem to be stuck in time.

The first ghost is someone the staff refers to as "Patrick," to honor all the Irish construction workers who built the armory. Patrick is full of mischief. Back in the 1980s, a group of Grays was doing some painting in the large entrance hall. The area they were working on was near the ceiling, so they had scaffolds set up, and all their paint was in small cups. The work was tedious, so at one point, they all took a break and headed upstairs to the mess hall. While they were sitting and talking, they heard someone rushing up the stairs. They called out to the latecomer. When they didn't get an answer, they all got up to see what was happening. That's when they heard someone rushing back down the stairs. Worried someone had broken in, they all ran downstairs and found a mess in the front hall. Someone or something had overturned all of the paint cups! It had to have just happened as they were running downstairs because the paint had not dripped off the scaffolding yet. The men thought that the mess had been made by

Patrick. Maybe Patrick did not approve of them taking a break and wanted to get them working again. But the joke was on Patrick because all the workers were too scared to finish painting that night.

Katrina, who was a previous director of the museum, and a member of the Grays, thought Patrick didn't like how she decorated the entryway. She had put a little table with a vase filled with flowers there. And she couldn't say how many times that vase was moved. She finally left it where Patrick put it, and it was never moved again!

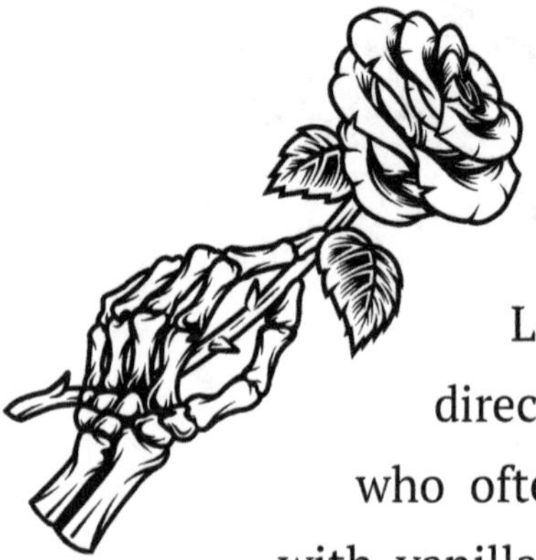

Another ghostly presence who has made himself known to the folks at Grays Armory is Major Lou Grosser. He was a past director of the Cleveland Grays who often liked to smoke a pipe with vanilla tobacco. The major took his job as director very seriously; he liked things done a certain way and kept the building in tiptop shape. One morning on his way to a meeting, the major had a heart attack and died on the floor of the drill hall. Since then, members swear they have smelled that pipe tobacco in the drill hall many times. They joke and say that the major sticks around to make sure that everything is being done correctly.

In one of the meeting rooms upstairs, there is a piano. Current Grays aren't sure how long it's been there or where it came from, but it seems to have come with its own ghost. Many people have reported seeing a woman in a white dress standing next to the piano like she is singing. Wouldn't it be great to catch one of her performances?

If you are brave enough to go down to the basement to the shooting range, you might encounter another ghost. People have told stories about hearing voices or seeing dark shadows move across the range. One member felt like someone was standing right behind them on the shooting range when they knew they were alone. The creepy feeling was bad enough, but when the member finished shooting and heard a voice call out, "Nice shot," that's when he ran out of the basement. He never goes to the basement range by himself anymore.

The staff has an exterminator come once a month, and one day, a new guy showed up to do the job. He ended up down in the shooting range by himself—or so he thought. The exterminator said the hair on the back of his neck stood up, and he felt like someone was standing behind him, almost breathing down his neck. When he turned around, the only thing he saw was a dark shadow that moved across the range. Chris, the current museum director, said the poor guy ran out so fast, he didn't even get his paperwork signed, and the next month, a new guy showed up to do the extermination work.

If you ever get a chance to tour Grays Armory and Museum, be on the lookout for the ghostly residents of the armory. Whatever you do, don't move the vase in the entryway, and if you smell vanilla tobacco smoke, you may want to cut your tour short!

The Cleveland Agora

The music venue known as the Cleveland Agora is huge in the music world. The Agora opened in 1966 in Little Italy as a place to showcase up-and-coming musical acts. In 1967, it moved to East Twenty-Fourth Street. A fire destroyed the East Twenty-Fourth Street location in 1986, and the Agora then moved to 5000 Euclid Avenue.

Constructed in 1913, the property at 5000 Euclid Avenue has been a vaudeville theater and a movie theater. The upstairs offices were home to some local radio stations, and the stage area upstairs was called the WHK Auditorium. This is the stage where disc jockey Alan Freed first used the words "rock and roll."

When the Cleveland Agora took over the space in the 1980s, live music came back—as did a lot of ghosts! The most famous ghost at the Agora is the man in the yellow coat. During a concert one night, a man was walking up the stairs when he tripped and spilled his drink. When he stood up, he felt cold all over, and the hair on the back of his neck stood up. He looked around, and there was a man in a yellow coat standing in front of him, shaking his head at him. The weird thing was that the man who tripped could see right through the man in the yellow coat! And just like that, the man in the yellow coat disappeared into thin air. The guy was pretty freaked out and left the show. The man said later he didn't feel like the man in the yellow coat wanted to hurt him and that he felt like it was a warning. And he hasn't been back to the Agora since!

In the late 1990s, a photographer was in the theater area taking pictures for an article about the Agora. He had asked the staff to stay out of that space until he was done so he didn't have to worry about getting unwanted people in his pictures. As he was taking pictures of the stage, he heard a door open and footsteps at the back of the theater. The photographer yelled out to whoever it was to give him a few more minutes. When he turned around, no one was there, and he hadn't heard the door open again. He shrugged it off and started taking pictures of the dance floor and the seats. When he raised his camera, he saw a woman sitting in the seats. The photographer asked her what she wanted, and she stood up. He noticed that she was wearing a fancy, old-fashioned dress. When he went to speak to her again, she vanished. The photographer ran out of the theater and right into the cleaning crew. When he told them his story, one of them said, "We used to see her all the time, but she leaves us alone now." The photographer left, but when he looked at his pictures, there was only a shadow where she had been sitting! Some people believe this ghostly woman is an actress who died in the building in the early 1900s. Whoever she is, people feel her presence in the main theater and in a room in the basement.

The Agora used to allow ghost hunting groups do investigations, and one night, a group came in to do an EVP (electronic voice phenomena) session. They were recording up on the catwalk (a structure high above the stage where lights are hung for concerts) when someone in the group started to feel really uncomfortable. He felt like someone was whispering in his ear, and it got so bad that they all went down to the stage. They listened to the recordings, but they didn't hear any answers to their questions. However, they did hear a woman whispering, "They are here. They need to get out. Get out." Do you know what they did next? They got out!

When we took tours to the Agora, it was amazing how many people's phone and camera batteries died while inside. However, when we got back outside, they would be fine. It was as if the spirits in the building were draining the energy from people's devices.

We are not sure who the ghosts are who haunt the Agora, but they definitely feel like the show must go on.

Squire's Castle

Squire's Castle

Located in the North Chagrin Reservation of the Cleveland Metroparks (Cleveland's extensive network of parks) is an abandoned mansion—Squire's Castle. Feargus Squire, an oil executive, bought 525 acres of land in what is now Willoughby Hills so he could build a country home to escape the city. He wanted a giant home where he could throw grand parties and entertain all of his wealthy friends.

When they started building in 1895, Feargus wanted to spend all his time on the estate, but his wife, Rebecca, really preferred city living. The more time she spent out in the country, the more unhappy she became. And the more unhappy she was, the less she slept.

Rebecca started wandering the house at night, carrying a red lantern to light her way.

One night, as the story goes, she was scared by something in the house. In her panic, she fell down the basement stairs, screaming as she went, and died. To this day, people claim that the ghost of Rebecca Squire can be seen wandering the gatehouse with a red lantern. Then a horrible scream is heard, and the light goes out.

That's a scary story, isn't it? There's only one problem: it's not true. Well, the part where it was built by Feargus Squire is true. However, Rebecca did not die in the house. It was never completed, and Feargus sold the property in 1922. Rebecca Squire died in 1929 in a home in Wickliffe, Ohio. Is it possible that Rebecca's spirit went back to a home that she didn't like when she was alive just to haunt it? And if it's not the ghost of Rebecca, then who is it?

I have heard many stories about people hearing screams and seeing the light from the red lantern moving through Squire's Castle. However, when I gave tours, I made sure people knew it was just a story. So can you imagine how shocked I was when people started showing me pictures and there were red orbs in them? It was terrifying, and I sure couldn't explain it!

On one tour, there was a man who made sure I knew he didn't believe in ghosts and that he only came on the tour because his wife wanted to go. I told the story about Squire's Castle while we were on the bus, and then I sent the group up to the castle in the dark. I was standing by the bus, waiting for people to come back, and the man who came to keep his wife company was the first person to come back to the bus. He was practically running down the path, and he looked like he had seen a ghost! He didn't say a word to me, so I asked his wife if he was okay. She started laughing and then replied, "He's fine. He was standing by the fireplace and thought I came up behind him and grabbed his arm. When he turned around, I was standing on the other side of the room, and now he's all freaked out." Needless to say, this man did not get off the bus at any of the other stops!

If you visit Squire's Castle, you may be lucky enough to see the red light of the lantern and hear the screams. We can't say who is doing the haunting, but it's guaranteed to give you goosebumps!

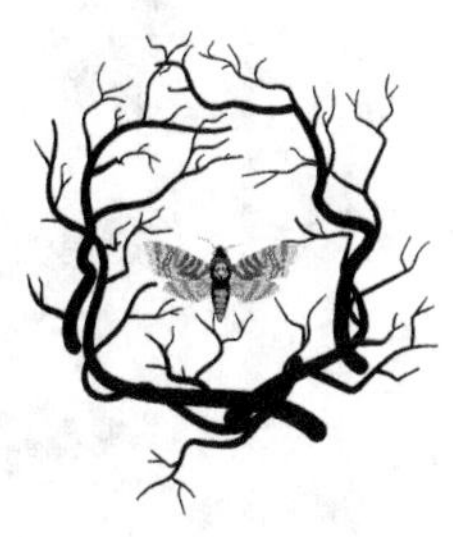

Old Fairport Harbor Lighthouse

Fairport Harbor Marine Museum and Lighthouse

If you take a thirty-five-minute drive east out of Cleveland, you will find yourself in Fairport Harbor, where the Grand River empties into Lake Erie.

Originally called Grandon, the town was laid out in 1812. The name of the town was changed to Fairport in 1836, and Harbor was added later.

The fifty-five-foot lighthouse was built in 1825 and one of eight lighthouses on the Great Lakes at the time. This lighthouse was not just a beacon for ships on Lake Erie, but also a light of hope and freedom for escaped slaves. The people of Fairport Harbor were abolitionists, and the city became one of the last stops on the Underground Railroad.

The lighthouse was replaced in 1871, and a new sixty-eight foot tower was built.

In 1917, a new lighthouse was built on the west break wall, and in 1925, the original light was extinguished. And in 1945, the Coast Guard turned the lighthouse over to the town.

Toward the end of World War II, there was talk of tearing down the lighthouse, but the town created the Fairport Harbor Historical Society to preserve the town's history and turn the lighthouse into the country's first marine museum.

I know, get to the scary stuff! To understand the ghosts who haunt the lighthouse you need to know who lived here in the beginning. In 1871, Captain Joseph Babcock was named head keeper of the lighthouse, and he brought his family to Fairport Harbor to live there. The family lived in the rooms on the second floor. Mrs. Mary Babcock was a sick woman and had to stay in bed quite a bit, so Captain Babcock gave her some cats to keep her company.

When she passed away, all of her cats seemed to disappear, except for one gray cat. This gray cat, named Sentinel, stayed at the lighthouse for many years, and there are some people who think he never left.

One former curator of the museum, Pam Brent, lived on the second floor for quite a while. She reported seeing a gray cat playing by the kitchen.

However, she didn't have a gray or any color cat! Pam says she has seen the ghostly feline playing throughout the house. One night, he jumped into bed with her—she could feel him lying by her leg but couldn't see him. Many of the museum volunteers and visitors say they have felt a phantom cat rubbing against their legs.

How strange is it the spirit of a cat stayed at the lighthouse all these years? The possible reason became clear when the trustees of the museum decided to have air conditioning installed. A worker had to crawl into a really tight space in the basement and then flip over onto his back. When he flipped over, he felt something under his head. Can you imagine how he felt when he saw the body of a mummified gray cat?

The Fairport Harbor Lighthouse has another spirit besides a ghost cat. People tell stories about a little ghost boy who haunts the lighthouse. While at the top of the lighthouse, people report hearing a little boy laughing. The Babcocks did have a little boy named Robbie, and he died while they lived in the lighthouse. Could the laughing ghost be the spirit of Robbie, a little boy just happy to be at the top of the lighthouse?

If you stop and visit the museum and lighthouse, I hope you're not allergic to ghost cats and you don't mind Robbie keeping you company on your tour. They both just want to make friends with their visitors.

William G. Mather Steamship

Around the Town Ghosts

A lot of times we hear ghost stories, but we can't always get into the places they haunt. Here are some great ghostly local legends.

The Drury Mansion

The Drury Mansion is on Euclid Avenue and was built for Francis Drury, who made his fortune in cast-iron stoves. The fifty-two room mansion, which was built in 1912, has a huge center staircase, towers that loom over an interior courtyard, and twisting hallways with rooms popping up off of them. Rumor has it there was even a tunnel that went underneath Euclid Avenue to the Drury Theater, which was built in 1914.

The house has changed hands many times since then. It has served as a boardinghouse and a home for girls, and in 1972, it was leased to the Ohio Adult Parole Authority and became a home for paroled prisoners.

You wouldn't think that prisoners would be afraid to live there, but many of them complained of groaning sounds, windows opening and closing on their own, doors that wouldn't stay closed, and footsteps echoing in empty hallways. Now a lot of these things are usually explained as plumbing sounds or the house settling, but there is one thing that can't be explained.

A staff member was walking up the main staircase, and he saw a woman in a long blue dress gliding toward him. And then she floated right through him and into the kitchen. As terrified as he was the first time he saw her, he got used to having her around and saw her in the kitchen a lot. It seemed to be her favorite place. He never figured out if she was a member of the Drury family or a spirit that decided to move into this amazing mansion.

The *William G. Mather* Steamship

The *William G. Mather* Steamship Museum is docked off the East Ninth Street Pier and is part of the Great Lakes Science Center. It is 618 feet long, almost the length of two football fields, and could carry fourteen thousand tons of cargo. Named for the president of the Cleveland-Cliffs Iron Company, the ship first launched in 1925. The *Mather* was in use until 1980, when it was taken out of service and became a museum.

We hadn't heard any ghost stories about the *Mather* until we spoke with the director. He told us that many of the volunteers working aboard the ship had some unexplained experiences. If they were in the area around the captain's cabin, they could hear children laughing and playing—the only thing missing were actual children!

Other volunteers have told stories about the ship's galley, which is the kitchen. After the galley was restored, they heard pots and pans clanging and men talking, as if a meal was being prepared. Out in the dining room, they have heard the chairs scraping on the floor, like people were sitting down to eat. The volunteers say it's almost as if the crew never left, staying on duty in the afterlife!

The Variety Theater

The Variety Theater located at 11817 Lorain Avenue on the west side opened Thanksgiving Day 1927. Like many theaters, it has been a movie theater, a vaudeville theater, and is now a live concert venue.

During a recent renovation, it seems that the work caused some of the ghosts to come to life, so to speak. It's believed that there are as many as ninety ghosts in the theater.

A woman in a white dress has been seen lingering around the ladies lounge and the water fountain on the first floor.

The shadowy figure of a man in an usher's uniform has been seen on the balcony. Some believe it is the spirit of an usher who worked there in the 1930s and actually died in one of the apartments attached to the theater.

Phantom workers have been heard working on the stage, and one of the ghosts is said to be a worker who died after falling off of a lighting scaffold.

One night, a ghost hunting group came in to do an investigation. During an EVP session, they heard a child laughing, so they put a teddy bear in a chair on the stage. They continued their investigation, and when they got back down to the stage, the teddy bear had been moved off the chair to the front of the stage. The ghost hunting group left the theater quickly, leaving the bear behind for the ghost.

These are some of my favorite haunted places in and around Cleveland, but there are many more. The amazing thing about all these ghost stories is how much history you can learn about a place while finding out about the ghosts that haunt them.

Ghost hunting is a great hobby for people who like history and are interested in the supernatural. And you can now do it with your phone and a few apps! Happy ghost hunting, and remember to follow the rules! Be respectful and courteous to any spirits you might meet, obey the law (no trespassing on private property), do no harm to public locations, and the most important rule is to be safe in your investigating!

I hope you enjoyed the spooky side of Cleveland!

Lifelong Cleveland resident **Beth A. Richards** has over a decade's worth of experience hosting Haunted Cleveland Ghost Tours. She is a history buff and researcher and loves to explore her hometown.

Check out some of the other Spooky America titles available now!

Spooky America was adapted from the creeptastic Haunted America series for adults. Haunted America explores historical haunts in cities and regions across America. Each book chronicles both the widely known and less-familiar history behind local ghosts and other unexplained mysteries. Here's more from *Haunted Cleveland* authors Beth A. Richards and Chuck L. Gove :

For more, visit HauntedCleveland.net.

www.ingramcontent.com/pod-product-compliance
Lightning Source LLC
La Vergne TN
LVHW010941100826
845153LV00002B/108
9781540249258